Original title:
Pineapple Paradise

Copyright © 2025 Creative Arts Management OÜ
All rights reserved.

Author: Samuel Kensington
ISBN HARDBACK: 978-1-80586-260-4
ISBN PAPERBACK: 978-1-80586-732-6

Canned Sunshine in a Jar

In a tropical grove where laughter flows,
Fruit with a crown in the sun brightly glows.
With a wink and a zest, it dances around,
A burst of sweet joy, just waiting to be found.

Jars lined up neatly, a golden parade,
Each slice a giggle, a jolly crusade.
Sticky solutions that ooze and they gleam,
A sugary laughter, like candy in a dream.

Mix them with soda, let bubbles take flight,
A fizzy concoction to sip day or night.
Each sip an adventure, each glance a delight,
A carnival of flavors, oh what a sight!

So gather your friends, let's feast in the sun,
With colors so vibrant, the joy's just begun.
In this jar of laughter, together we sway,
Chasing life's worries, just splashing away!

Crowned Delight

In the jungle, sweet and bright,
Fruity hats in morning light.
Dancing squirrels, all astound,
Giggling, twirling all around.

Banana shoes and mango crowns,
Jumpy monkeys, silly frowns.
Piney hats that wiggle fast,
Joyful laughter, always cast.

Harvest of Joy

Gather round for fruity fun,
Sunshine smiles, let's all run.
Juicy treats all piled high,
Tickle fights beneath the sky.

Baskets bursting, laughter peals,
Wacky hats and silly heels.
Every bite a laugh, hooray!
Fruity fun is here to stay.

An Ember of Piney Whispers

In a grove of giggling dreams,
Fruits are bursting at the seams.
Whispers soft of tangy tales,
Where the laughter never fails.

Frogs in shades and buzzing bees,
Join the party, if you please.
Shadow dances, sunshine winks,
Joyful tunes in varied links.

The Tropic's Kiss

Underneath a breezy sky,
Coconuts that wink and sigh.
Sweaty brows and sunburnt skin,
Guess it's fun to let them in.

Splashing waves and playful cheers,
Silliness throughout the years.
Sippin' punch with whipped up dreams,
Laughter floats on tropical streams.

Flavorful Echoes of a Tropical Breeze

In a land where the fruit wears a crown,
Laughter rings as we tumble down.
Sipping juice like a dancing fool,
Sticky fingers, oh how cool!

Coconuts wiggle on sandy shores,
Waves erupt, opening doors.
The sun tickles our cheeks so round,
In this tropic, joy is found.

Moonlit Harvests by the Sea

Under the stars with a fruity delight,
We giggle and sing into the night.
A harvest of laughter, sweet and bright,
Banana peels slipping, what a sight!

The waves join in with a splash and a cheer,
Dancing with crabs, never show fear.
With each twirl and a slosh we agree,
This moonlit feast is wild and free.

Sun-Drenched Joy

Golden rays tickle our skin with glee,
Every bite bursts like a fiesta to me.
Surrounded by friends, we laugh and we play,
Fruit masques on faces, come join the fray!

The breeze carries jokes from palm to palm,
Every sip of sunshine feels like a balm.
With each juicy morsel, we sing with mirth,
In this sun-soaked land, we find our worth.

Tropical Dreams in Edible Gold

In a grove where the colors collide,
A treasure of sweetness we can't hide.
Joking with parrots, we eat without care,
An orchard of giggles fills the air.

With each tasty slice, the laughter grows loud,
Fruits in our hands, we're feeling so proud.
The flavor parade struts along the trail,
In this edible world, we'll never fail.

Rich Bounty of the Sun

In a land where sunshine beams,
Fruit wears crowns and giggles in dreams.
Jungle jesters wear green suits,
With fruit-filled hats and dancing boots.

Juicy smiles upon each slice,
Sweetness drips, oh, isn't it nice?
Laughter bubbles with every bite,
In a feast that feels just right.

The Fruit That Dances

Twirling fruit with sunny flair,
Wobbling bodies, without a care.
With a rhythm that makes you cheer,
They shimmy close, oh, come near!

Hula skirts and straw hats sway,
Inviting all to join the play.
With fruit-salad breaks and punches cool,
It's a party, let's all drool!

Swaying Palms and Sweet Nectar

Palm trees sway, a funny sight,
Shaking hands in sheer delight.
Beneath them, a sticky treat,
Offers laughter, oh so sweet.

Juicy drops like a river flow,
With nectar sweet, the fun won't slow.
Sip and giggle, that's our aim,
In this tropical, wild game.

Echoes of Tropical Splendor

In the distance, echoes burst,
Fruitful giggles, quenched our thirst.
Comedy blooms in sandy cracks,
With humor packed in juicy sacks.

Laughter's ripe with every bite,
The sunshine gives a golden light.
Oh, the joy of this weird place,
Where fruits wear smiles, just for grace.

Citrus Dreams and Ocean Breezes

In a land where fruits wear crowns,
Laughter bounces off the towns.
Sunshine dances on bright leaves,
Where even seaweed giggles, it weaves.

Juicy drips down sunlit cheeks,
Silly seagulls play hide-and-seeks.
A splash of zest, a twist of rhyme,
In citrus dreams, we have a good time.

Island Whispers in the Breeze

Whispers float on breezy shores,
Where the fruit sings, and laughter roars.
Coconuts chuckle in the palms,
And sticky hands bring fruit-filled charms.

Sandy toes and fruity hats,
A parade of giggling chubby cats.
As sunlight winks, the waves all cheer,
A frolic where the skies are clear.

A Slice of Heaven

A bright slice of joy on a sunny plate,
Where everything's ripe, not a moment late.
Smiles mix with flavors so sweet,
A culinary dance that can't be beat.

Sprinkled with fun, just like confetti,
It's a party where no one's petty.
With each bite, a giggle grows,
In this garden where silliness flows.

The Lush Fruit Symphony

Orchestra of colors, a fruity delight,
Mangoes jiggle, and berries take flight.
In harmony, they prank the day,
Each note a laugh, in their own fun way.

Pluck a banana, hear the jest,
The grapes join in, they're simply the best.
With every crunch and juicy cheer,
This lush symphony brings everyone near.

Vibrant Sun-Drenched Delights

A fruit in a crown, so bright and so bold,
Its spiky attire, a sight to behold.
Juicy surprise, with flavors so grand,
It slips from my grip, like a slippery band.

Sweeter than dreams, oh blissful delight,
I wore it for lunch, quite a comical sight.
Sunkissed and laughing, the juice drips and flows,
As I slide on the grass, what a sticky pose!

Ethereal Essence of the Grove

In a grove where the laughter and sunshine collide,
A fruit with a grin, like a joker's glide.
With shades of bright yellow and green all around,
It dances with joy, oh what fun to be found!

I cut it up nicely, but it jumps off the plate,
Rolling away, oh fruit, don't tempt fate!
Chasing it down, with a giggle and cheer,
Is this a feast, or a comedic frontier?

Sweetness in the Shade

Underneath the sun, in the shade I reside,
With a slice of a treat, what a fruity pride!
I take a big bite, and it squirts on my nose,
With laughter erupting, all my friends know.

Sticky fingers flying, a party of taste,
In this goofy jungle, no second is waste.
With giggles aplenty and flavors galore,
This fruity explosion keeps us wanting more!

Memories of Sunny Breezes

A tropical burst, bright memories swirl,
With laughter so sweet, it gives life a twirl.
Chasing a fruit in a brilliant parade,
We're all on a quest, but our plans start to fade.

With juice on our shirts and gum in our hair,
We giggle and run, without a single care.
The fruit rolls away, we just can't contain,
These moments of fun, we'll forever retain!

Serenity Under the Canopy

Underneath the leafy shade,
Laughter bubbles in the glade.
A squirrel with a fruity hat,
Dances by the chatty cat.

Juicy drops from trees cascade,
While goofy monkeys serenade.
The breeze is sweet, a tropical tease,
As we swing and sway with ease.

A Feast of the Tropics

Table set with colors bright,
Flavors clash, a pure delight.
Sticky fingers, faces smeared,
Belly laughs, just as we cheered.

Tasty bites from nature's hand,
Lemons, limes—oh isn't it grand?
Food fights break amidst the cheer,
Whoops! There goes another beer!

Whispering Shores of Satisfaction

Waves that giggle on the sand,
Tickle toes, how very grand!
Footprints leading to the sun,
Every splash is so much fun.

Shells that giggle, crabs that dance,
Each misstep is a second chance.
Seagulls dive and swoop around,
Funnies found where joy is found.

The Coastal Retreat

In a hammock, softly swayed,
A drink in hand, I'm blissfully laid.
Tropical birds sing silly tunes,
While sunbeams play like playful loons.

A coconut rolls, and I just laugh,
Trying to catch it—oh what a gaffe!
Nature's playground shines so bright,
Turning every moment into sheer delight.

Morning Glory in Tropical Skies

In the dawn's warm light, they sway,
Funky hats on their heads, what a display.
Sipping juice with tiny straws,
Laughter rings out, oh, the applause!

Bouncing in the breeze, their dance refined,
Feet in the sand, leave worries behind.
With funny shades and smiles wide,
Who knew the day would be such a ride?

Twirling to the rhythm, they sing bold,
A chorus of colors, a sight to behold.
Squirrels in shades join the fun,
Mirth in the air, the day's just begun!

Beneath the sun, where the giggles flow,
Under palm trees, watch the antics grow.
With every sip of sweetness divine,
This morning's glory is simply sublime!

A Golden Retreat

In a land where the sun reigns supreme,
Lives a fruit that feels like a dream.
It's golden and juicy, with such flair,
You'd think it wears a crown, quite rare!

Fruits dress in hula skirts, so chic,
Making jokes every day of the week.
With every bite a chuckle bursts,
Who knew sweet could quench such thirsts?

Tangs of humor in every bite,
Tickling taste buds, morning delight.
They hold a feast, all friends unite,
Sipping laughter till the stars ignite!

This retreat is paradise in disguise,
Sharing jokes and bliss under sunny skies.
In a golden glow, where giggles zoom,
Every corner sparkles, joy in bloom!

Celebrating Sweet Joys

Underneath the warm sun's balmy glow,
A party forms, watch the laughter flow.
With tiny hats and drinks in hands,
They toast to silliness in these lands!

Fruits piled high, a vibrant mountain,
Life's little joys pour like a fountain.
A ticklish breeze, funny tales shared,
Every smile, another joy declared!

Join the conga line, wobbly and grand,
The fruit brigade waves, a cheerful band.
Squirrels dance like they've just won gold,
In this sweet fest, happiness unfolds!

With every chuckle and every cheer,
The day grows brighter, far and near.
Celebrating the joys, let hopes rise,
In this carnival of fruit, life's a surprise!

In the Embrace of Island Trees

Under the trees where the coconuts sway,
Tropical magic brightens the day.
In costumes made of leaves, oh so fine,
They giggle and dance, sipping sunshine!

The waves tickle toes, laughter in the air,
As squirrels in tuxedos join this affair.
With fruity snacks and a treasure map,
Funny antics unfold—take a nap!

Bouncing high, they mimic the breeze,
Together they waltz, a joyous freeze.
Silly stories shared beneath their shade,
In the embrace of trees, fun never fades!

With hearts light as feathers, all troubles shrink,
In this embrace, just giggle and think.
Of days filled with joy, forever crowned,
Nature's jesters, laughter unbound!

Beneath the Tropical Canopy

Under leafy trees so wide,
I found a fruit, my secret guide.
The locals laugh, they call it gold,
A spiky crown, it's bold and old.

With juice that drips and smiles that beam,
I dance along this fruity dream.
The sweetness makes me sing and shout,
In this wild jungle, there's no doubt!

Slices of Summer

A slice so juicy, it slips my grip,
I chase it down, what a funny trip!
Giggles wrap around my waist,
As I dive into this fruity taste.

Laughter floats on the ocean breeze,
While fruit flies dance among the trees.
Who needs a boat? Just grab a slice,
And sail away on fruity spice!

A Serenade of Sunshine

With every bite, a tingle bright,
It sings to me in pure delight.
The sun shines down, oh what a show,
As I hum along, my spirits grow.

Every spit of seeds that flies,
Brings on more laughs, oh how time flies!
An ode to fruit, my giggly muse,
In this sweet world, I can't refuse!

The Essence of Island Bliss

In a hammock swinging, it's paradise,
With fruit that smiles, oh how nice!
I take a sip, the flavors burst,
This blissful moment, I'm well-versed.

As waves crash down, I chuckle loud,
With every sip, I feel so proud.
A fruit that's funny, oh so sweet,
In this bliss, my heart skips a beat!

Island Essence

On the shore where coconuts sway,
Laughter greets the bright sun's ray.
A fruit parade on sandy feet,
Tropical treats, oh what a feat!

Jellyfish doing the conga line,
Dancing with mangoes, oh so fine.
Pineapples wearing shades so cool,
They rule the beach, the fruity school!

A Symphony of Tropic Fruits

Oranges sing in citrus tones,
While bananas dance like silly clones.
Grapes roll by with tiny hats,
A fruity band amidst the chats!

Coconuts strum their hairy shells,
Berries giggle in happy spells.
A pineapple's prank, a splash in the sea,
These fruity friends, so wild and free!

Gardens of Sunshine

In gardens where the papayas play,
The sunlight shines a golden ray.
Beneath a mango tree so lush,
A fruit salad forms with a funny hush.

Watermelons roll down the lane,
Silly raccoons join the fun, oh what a gain!
Lemons giggle, sour but bright,
In this garden, all is just right!

At the Heart of a Fruitful Realm

At dawn, the fruits begin to chatter,
A kiwi's joke makes everyone splatter.
Passion fruits twirl in the breeze,
While sunflowers sway with utmost ease.

Limes compete with lemons in jest,
A fruity showdown, who is the best?
The laughter echoes through the trees,
In this realm, joy comes with ease!

Sun-Kissed Lushness

In the land where sunshine hides,
Fruits wear crowns, like silly guides.
Coconut laughs on the sandy shore,
While mango dances, wanting more.

Bananas giggle, hanging high,
Making jokes as the parrots fly.
Lemonade rivers flow with zest,
In this jungle, we simply jest.

Lushness sways with a playful breeze,
Palm trees wink, do as they please.
Every smoothie speaks of cheer,
In the heart, we've got the gear.

So let's toast with a fruity cheer,
Life's too short, let's shift the gear.
In a world where laughter reigns,
Sun-kissed dreams, oh, what remains!

Juicy Dreams in the Tropics

In a fruit bowl, the antics roam,
Tropical friends call this place home.
Passion fruit sings a love song sweet,
While watermelon wiggles to the beat.

Lime slips down, slippery and sly,
Chasing sweet tarts as they fly by.
Under the sun, they're all a gem,
Tasting joy, just like a dream.

Cactus sneers at prickly pears,
Sharing secrets without any cares.
Tiki torches laugh with delight,
As each fruit has its own spotlight.

Boys and girls with juicy grins,
Jump in the chaos where fun begins.
In the tropics, we let dreams pop,
With every bite, we just can't stop!

Golden Fruit Reverie

Golden treasures hang overhead,
Faces of bananas playfully spread.
Citrus dances with a twist and turn,
In this realm, our hearts just burn.

Tangerine dreams sprout on the vine,
As papaya whispers, 'Life is fine.'
Grapefruits giggle, juggling bright,
In this garden, the mood's just right.

Surrounded by colors, bold and bright,
Every slice brings pure delight.
Fruits chatter in a joyful spree,
Creating tales of fruity glee.

Sipping nectar like a crown,
On these waves, we never drown.
With laughter ripe, we take a swing,
In fruity reverie, we sing!

Oasis of Flavor

In an oasis where flavors collide,
Watermelon winks with juicy pride.
Kiwi croons a sweet serenade,
While pineapple dreams in soft shade.

Mangoes twirl like they're on ice,
Grapes roll by, oh, so nice.
Every bite, a burst of cheer,
In this land, we shed our fear.

Coconut sways to the sunlit beat,
Limes jump out, they can't be beat.
In the laughter of each small treat,
The flavor oasis can't be beat.

Peachy keen, they smile and play,
Making every dull moment sway.
With every splash and fruity jest,
This is where we feel our best!

Sunlit Shores of Bliss

On sandy shores where laughter rings,
The fruit of joy, oh how it sings!
With shades of green and bursts of gold,
A merry feast for young and old.

We dance and twirl in sunshine bright,
With slippery slices, what a sight!
A fruity splash here, a zesty shoe,
Who knew a snack could wheeze and moo?

Catch the waves, let worries float,
In juicy dreams, we sip and gloat!
With every bite, a giggle's spread,
Who thought a fruit could moonwalk, instead?

As sunsets paint the sky with cheer,
We toast to flavors far and near.
In this tropical bliss, we find our way,
To frolic and feast day after day.

Juicy Adventures in the Tropics

In the land where the sunshine beams,
Every fruit spouts wild, silly dreams.
With juice that splatters, laughing so,
A tropical party, let's start the show!

Adventurers roam with cups in hand,
Mixing flavors, oh isn't it grand?
A splash of surprise, a twist of fun,
Who knew juice could have such run?

From trees so tall, they look to jest,
Their fruity antics top all the rest.
With every sip, we snicker and laugh,
Creating memories on our juicy path.

So grab your friends, let's share this thrill,
In nature's bounty, we find our fill.
With laughter ringing through our days,
Juicy adventures in zesty ways.

Under the Canopy of Sunlight

In shadows cast by leaves so wide,
We gather 'round with fruit as our guide.
The sun above, a playful tease,
As we munch on treasure 'neath swaying trees.

With giggles bright and smiles so sweet,
Nature's candy is quite the treat!
Dancing fruits from branches sway,
Can you catch one? Oh, what a play!

The breeze it rustles, what a fun dance,
As we engage in a snack-filled trance.
With zesty laughter and twinkling eyes,
Every bite leads to silly surprise.

So stay awhile beneath this hue,
With fruity magic and friends like you.
Under the spotlight of daylight's gleam,
We confess that we're living the dream!

Golden Fruit and Rustling Palms

With palms a-sway and giggles wide,
Grab the golden fruit, let's take a ride!
Laughter echoes, the juice will flow,
A fruity whirlwind, here we go!

Beneath the trees, we start to play,
Who can balance without a sway?
With fruity laughter, we take our shot,
Who knew snacks could end up a plot?

Sipping from coconuts, feeling fine,
With every chic bite, we draw the line.
In this paradise of zest and cheer,
Every moment is deliciously clear.

So let the rustling palms be our song,
In this wild world, where we belong.
Golden fruit brings fun to the scene,
And every trail leads to a dream.

Uplifted by Nature's Bounty

In a world where fruits might dance,
A citrus twist, a jolly chance.
With laughter bursting, flavor bright,
We sip on joy, our hearts take flight.

Bananas wearing silly hats,
Coconuts with chattering chats.
The mangoes tease with every bite,
While every taste brings pure delight.

The sun bestows a golden glow,
As fruity breezes softly blow.
In nature's joke, we leap and sway,
Embraced by bounty, come what may.

With every slice, a silly grin,
In this fun orchard, we all win.
So here's to nature's funny flair,
In fruit-filled joy, we love to share.

An Eden by the Sea

Where coconuts hold secret dreams,
And seaweed dances in sunbeams.
A beach where fruits play hide and seek,
While waves tickle with laughter's peak.

A pineapple with shades so cool,
Sipping juice right by the pool.
The mango giggles, ripe and loud,
As sun-kissed fruits form a happy crowd.

Starfish join in fruit parade,
While seashells hum a soft charade.
In this watery fiesta bright,
Lifesavers made of pure delight.

With smoothies swirling like the tide,
In glasses where our giggles hide.
An Eden made of fruity fun,
A place where joy is never done.

Lustrous Shores and Tropical Treats

On shining shores where colors pop,
Fragrant bites that make us hop.
With juicy laughter in the air,
Every nibble is beyond compare.

A grapefruit wearing polka dots,
And handstands from a bunch of nuts.
The cherries giggle, berries sway,
Come join the fun, don't walk away.

The tides bring whispers from the trees,
Where coconut dreams float on the breeze.
We feast on treats that dance and play,
In this kooky beachside cabaret.

With every wave, a juicy jest,
Nature's laughter is the best.
So taste the sun and let it shine,
These playful fruits are truly divine!

The Aroma of Sunlit Fruits

A fragrant breeze of joyful bliss,
Where lemons smile and fruits kiss.
With every scent, a chuckle flows,
As sunlight drips from mango toes.

The oranges jive, the grapefruits sing,
Dancing together in a ring.
Banana peels create a slide,
As laughter rolls with every tide.

In every corner, flavors tease,
With tangerine whispers in the breeze.
A fruity laughter, bold and free,
In the day's sun, we just let be.

So come and join this fruit parade,
With every slice, a new escapade.
Life is sweet, with every chew,
In sunlit bliss, dreams all come true.

Cotton Candy Hues of Tropic Dreams

In a land where the sun wears a grin,
Fruits dance under a sky made of gin.
Laughter bubbles in the warm ocean spray,
As coconuts play hopscotch all day.

Colors melting like a sweet candy floss,
Bananas gossip, they're never at a loss.
Puffy clouds float with a giggle and sway,
While seagulls joke, chasing worries away.

Ferns and Fruits in a Coastal Haven

Ferns wave hello, in a playful breeze,
Mangoes exchange their jokes with the trees.
Watermelon splashes in a game of tag,
While pineapples wear hats, looking quite rag.

Coconuts chuckle, oh what a sight,
In this silly garden where all is right.
Limes fight lemons in a citrus brawl,
As laughter rolls in, summer's grand ball.

Tales of an Endless Summer

Flip-flops flapping on sandy terrain,
Sunscreen goofs, leaving a funny stain.
Ice cream drips, a sad little fate,
While crabs dance on their pincers, so great.

Each sunset giggles, painting the sky,
As tropical birds learn to dance and fly.
A parrot jokes over fruity delight,
In this endless summer, full of pure light.

Tropical Sweetness

Gummy bears tumble from the palm trees high,
While jellybeans bounce like clouds in the sky.
A sugar rush rolls on a coconut wave,
And every sip's sweeter, cheers to the brave.

In this land of candy, where fruits wear a grin,
Silly mangoes and limes dance just to win.
With each twist and turn, fun's always in sight,
In the tropical sweetness, laughter ignites!

Dancing with Sunshine

Beneath the bright and cheery sky,
We twirl and spin, oh me, oh my!
With laughter ringing in the breeze,
We shake our hips with such great ease.

The sunbeams dance upon our heads,
While mischief springs from leafy beds.
With every twirl, a giggle soars,
As silly games lead to uproars.

Coconuts fall with splashes loud,
Our antics leave us feeling proud.
We sip sweet drinks that drip with glee,
And race the waves to feel so free.

Each moment's bright, a joyful theme,
As we embrace our sunlit dream.
And with each step, our spirits rise,
In this dance beneath the skies!

Blissful Golden Kingdom

In a land where laughter reigns,
Golden fruits ease all our pains.
We wear our crowns of leafy bliss,
And steal the day with every kiss.

The breeze carries sweet jokes to share,
As we lounge without a care.
Silly hats sit on our heads,
While we nap on cozy beds.

Banana boots and mango ties,
We waddle by with goofy sighs.
Our joyful hearts beat wild and fast,
In this kingdom, fun's unsurpassed.

With every giggle, laughter flies,
Creating joy that never dies.
Embracing silliness divine,
In our golden realm, we shine!

Sweet Memories in the Tropics

In the tropics, where dreams take flight,
We gather 'round with hearts so light.
Sticky fingers and sweet, sweet treats,
While dancing on the sandy streets.

Funny stories shared with glee,
Each wave's a laugh, just wait and see!
We slip and slide, it's quite a show,
As our joy begins to flow.

With sticky hugs and sunny smiles,
We walk on sunshine for a while.
Our hearts are full, it's plain to see,
These memories crafted happily.

We sip on drinks with colorful hues,
And celebrate silly, wild views.
In the soil of laughter so sweet,
Our bonds grow strong with every beat!

Aromas of Coastal Delight

The ocean breeze carries scents so fine,
Mixing with laughter, oh how they entwine!
Salty air and sweet treats collide,
As we bounce like waves on a joyous ride.

We bake our dreams in the warm sun's glow,
With every giggle, we steal the show.
Mischievous seagulls dance in flight,
While our antics spark a silly light.

Coconut hats and whimsical shoes,
We prance along with vibrant hues.
Our hearts skip beats with every sound,
Creating laughter where joy is found.

With aromas that tickle our nose,
We feast on fun as the cool wind blows.
Each moment savored, a sweet delight,
In this coastal haven, everything's bright!

Tasting the Sunlit Horizon

A fruit so bright, it wears a crown,
In mockery, it won't back down.
Juicy bits, the taste of glee,
Sipping sunshine by the sea.

With laughter loud and sunburned toes,
Beneath the shade where breeze just blows.
Squirty juice, a sticky fight,
We're delighted with each bite.

From smoothies thick to cakes that rise,
It's a feast that breaks all ties.
A quirky snack, it can't be tamed,
In fruit contests, it's well-named.

So grab a slice and share the fun,
In this sweet game, we've already won.
With joy that dances on our tongues,
Here's to laughter, life, and puns!

Isle of Sweet Surrender

On this isle, so bright and bold,
We trade our worries for some gold.
Ripened smiles, a zesty taste,
No sip of sorrow goes to waste.

Tropical drinks with little umbrellas,
Jokes on each other, like silly fella.
The more we drink, the more we cheer,
With giggles echoing throughout the year.

Coconuts knock and laugh aloud,
As we dance beneath the cloud.
Lay back, relax, it's all a dream,
In sunshine's glow, we reign supreme.

Mango mambo with a twist of lime,
These fruity rhythms, they're simply sublime.
A place where sweetness sets us free,
In our paradise of carefree glee.

Vibrant Days Beneath the Tropics

Beneath the sun, we twirl and spin,
Where every day feels like a win.
Bananas slip, coconuts roll,
In vibrant hues, we find our soul.

Giggles rise like waves on shore,
As we dive into a fruit-filled lore.
Carving laughter in the sand,
Sketching dreams that feel so grand.

With grinning faces, we gather round,
In fruit-faced games, our joys abound.
A fruity feast that never ends,
With silly tales, we'll make amends.

So here we toast with tropical cheer,
As fruity frolics draw us near.
In this kaleidoscope of the sweet,
Every moment's a tasty treat!

Days of Joy and Coconut Dreams

Under the palms, we kick our feet,
Each coconut's a special treat.
We crack them open with a cheer,
With every splash, we're free from fear.

Floating rafts and laughter loud,
In this paradise, we're so proud.
Bananas play peek-a-boo,
Our joy's a tide that grows anew.

In a whirl of sunshine, we concoct,
Silly moments, we can't be blocked.
A dance-off with the ocean breeze,
While sipping juice that brings us ease.

So let the waves drift us away,
In sunny laughter, let us stay.
Together here, we make our scene,
In joyous days and coconut dreams!

Blossoms of Summer's Embrace

In a land of golden delight,
Where the sun shines day and night,
Fruits wear crowns of spiky cheer,
And laughter dances in the air.

Whimsical winds blow through the trees,
Tickled by the buzzing bees,
Juicy morsels, oh what a sight,
In this realm of pure delight.

The grass is green, the skies are blue,
With giggles from the vibrant crew,
As we munch on the treasures tucked,
In this feast, we can't get stuck!

So raise a toast with fruity drinks,
In this paradise, the fun never stinks,
For with every sweet and tangy bite,
We embrace the summer's silly light.

Finding Paradise Beneath the Sun

Underneath the blazing beam,
We discover nature's dream,
Laughter bubbles like a brook,
As we dance, a joyful nook.

Straw hats wobble on our heads,
While sweet fruit juice spills like threads,
The sunbeams tickle at our toes,
As we sway where the breeze flows.

Wobbly tables filled with treats,
Silly clowns and dancing feats,
In this sunlit, wacky place,
Every moment's filled with grace.

So let's sing songs of silly glee,
Where worries fade, and all are free,
In our hands, the day's bright fun,
Chasing shadows 'til we're done.

Warm Embrace of Nature's Gifts

Fluffy clouds above us float,
With a magical, wobbly boat,
Set sail on a sea of pure cheer,
While fruity smiles draw us near.

Laughter erupts like fizzy drinks,
As we plop on soft, juicy kinks,
With flavors bursting all around,
In this bliss, pure joy is found.

Bumbling buddies spill their snacks,
On a path where giggles stack,
With every slice and every grin,
Nature knows just where to begin.

So let's twirl beneath the trees,
With dance moves that aim to please,
In this embrace of warm delight,
Every moment feels just right.

A Slice of Tropical Ecstasy

In a tropic dream where flavors bloom,
The laughter echoes through the room,
A slice here, a bite so grand,
Mirth is washed up on the sand.

Grinning faces, all aglow,
With treats that dance and juice that flows,
Every crunch a silly song,
As we feast and laugh along.

The sun is hot, our hearts are light,
We twirl and giggle, pure delight,
With every shared and playful tease,
Joy just slips along the breeze.

So come and join this fruity flair,
In this place, there's love to share,
With every slice, we find our beat,
In a world so wild and sweet.

A Symphony of Citrus

In a land where fruits wear crowns,
Laughter dances all around,
Oranges play the sweetest tunes,
Lemons make the silliest sounds.

Citrus friends on a vibrant stage,
Grapefruits twirl in a zesty rage,
Limes crack jokes with playful zest,
Bananas wink, they're the very best!

Sunshine drips from the chandeliers,
Mangoes juggle, while everyone cheers,
Papayas sing with tango flair,
In this fruity world, we shed all care!

So join the feast, come take a ride,
In the zest-filled moonlight by the tide,
With every bite, a laugh we share,
In this citrus land, beyond compare!

Glorious Garden of Delights

In a garden where the colors blend,
Fruits argue over who's the trend,
Berries pout, big peaches strut,
While kiwi shows off its fuzzy gut.

The cherries giggle, swinging low,
While strawberries put on a show,
Grapes are stacked in towers tall,
But one bad fall—oh, what a sprawl!

The watermelon takes a lazy roll,
Dreaming of a comedy patrol,
While the cantaloupe cracks wise in cheer,
Making the other fruits disappear!

In this garden, joy's a breeze,
Every fruit dances with such ease,
With laughter sprouting from each vine,
In this colorful realm, all is fine!

Twilight Tunes of the Tropics

As the sun dips low, the fruits convene,
Under the stars, there's a vibrant scene,
Pineapples sway with a funky beat,
While coconuts bring the disco heat.

Mangoes spin like they're in a trance,
With every twist, they take a chance,
Bananarama leads the dance tonight,
Making monkeys move with pure delight.

The starfruit glimmers with playful pride,
While grapefruits roll down a juicy slide,
Papayas giggle, wearing shades so bright,
In this tropical night, everything's right!

So join the chorus, sing out loud,
In this fruity fiesta, we're all so proud,
With laughter ringing through the air,
In twilight tunes, there's joy to share!

Fields of Sunlight Fruit

In fields where the fruits bask in the sun,
All day long, they just have fun,
Cherries race on strawberry trails,
While the elderberries tell funny tales.

Lemons in sunglasses plot a scheme,
Watching the peaches, they giggle and gleam,
The pumpkins roll with laughter so light,
As they play in the soft moonlight.

Watermelons bounce on grassy hills,
Spinach throws in some quirky thrills,
While bananas wave as they pass on by,
Joy fills the air, oh me, oh my!

So skip through these fields, come and explore,
With fruits that laugh and never bore,
In this vibrant world, let's dance and sing,
For in these fruity fields, joy is king!

Bright Paths Through Golden Fields

In fields of gold where pineapples lay,
Squirrels dance in a fruity ballet.
A smoothie spills, oh what a sight,
Laughter echoes, pure delight.

The sun shines bright, hats on our heads,
With juicy laughs, we fill our spreads.
Umbrellas shade our silly games,
We toss the fruit and call out names.

Straw hats wobble, folks on the run,
Tripping over joy, oh what fun!
Golden drips on our chinny-chin,
While sun and giggles start to spin.

So grab a slice, come take a seat,
In this fun spot, life's a treat.
Under blue skies, we find our bliss,
In a sticky, sweet, fruity kiss.

Hidden Treasures of Juiciness

Deep in the grove where sweet things grow,
Hidden treasures begin to glow.
Beneath the leaves, a fruity find,
With laughter loud and hearts so kind.

Giggling friends with juice on their face,
Chasing raindrops—what a race!
A bounty brought from nature's well,
Sips of laughter—do you hear that yell?

Coconuts crash like clowns on cue,
While sticky fingers try to chew.
Sweet explosions, oh what a roar,
We chew and chomp, then ask for more!

Under the sun, we munch and glow,
Savor each sip of the golden flow.
The secret's out, oh what a thrill,
Juicy treasures, our hearts do fill!

Sweet Tides of the Tropics

On tropical shores where laughter sings,
Waves so funny, they bring their flings.
Coconut kings, with crowns so bright,
Stomp through sand, what a silly sight!

Sipping drinks from pineapple cups,
Conversations fly like playful pups.
Ocean breezes dance through the air,
As we giggle without a care.

Bright flip-flops squawk like a parade,
Tumbling laughter—we're all dismayed.
With every wave, a giggle is tossed,
In this sweet tide, we find the lost.

So we'll ride the waves, come laugh with me,
On sandy shores, wild and free.
The tropics call, let's jump right in,
With laughter and joy, let the fun begin!

Cherishing Every Golden Moment

In the sunshine's glow, we take our stand,
With juicy joy that's truly grand.
Belly laughs and silly grins,
These golden moments, where joy begins.

Gather 'round, let stories unfold,
About fluff and fruit and the brave and bold.
Each bite savored, every giggle caught,
In this golden world of joy we've sought.

We jump and skip on the golden shore,
With sticky hugs that make us roar.
Cherishing each laugh, we bask in glee,
These moments together, just you and me.

So raise your slice, it's time to cheer,
For every giggle whispered near.
In our golden treasure of sweet delight,
We dance with joy, all day and night!

Tropical Reverie

In a land where fruits wear crowns,
Sunshine dances, never frowns.
Coconuts giggle, mangoes wink,
Laughter flows with every drink.

Bikini-clad crabs do the cha-cha,
While parrots sing in bizarre ha-ha.
Flip-flops flop in joyful tunes,
Even the sun wears silly balloons.

Sun-Kissed Tropics

The palm trees sway in a ballet,
As iguanas prance and play.
Sandcastles rise, then tumble down,
With hermit crabs wearing tiny crowns.

Oceans splash with a cheeky grin,
Seagulls dive in a playful spin.
Beach balls bounce, a bright parade,
Mistaken for a dolphin's escapade.

Golden Juices of Summer

Sipping nectar on the shore,
Sticky fingers, but who keeps score?
Juicy laughter fills the air,
As sunburned noses take the dare.

Watermelon slices in a heap,
A feast that's fit for friends who leap.
Hold your drink, it spritzed again!
We toast to summer's funny gain.

The Orchard of Sweet Delights

In a grove where sweetness reigns,
Fruit does twist and dance like trains.
Carts are loaded, giggles fly,
Strawberry cheeks and pie in the sky.

Cherries play hide and seek with zest,
While oranges don their Sunday best.
The harvest moon wears a silly hat,
And laughter grows in each grassy mat.

Tidal Waves of Sweetness

In a land where fruit is king,
Laughter dances on the swing.
Juicy nuggets in the sun,
Sipping sunshine—oh, what fun!

Sticky fingers, giggles loud,
We parade, a merry crowd.
Tasting joy with every bite,
Sandy toes, the mood's just right.

Mangoes blush, they seem to tease,
Belly laughs in the warm breeze.
Coconuts play hide and seek,
Sweetened smiles, no need to speak.

This fruity feast, a sunlit show,
So many flavors in a row.
As waves crash, we'll sing and sway,
In our sweet, bright getaway.

Splashes of Golden Bliss

In a splash of sun-kissed cheer,
Golden fruit brings joy near.
Waves of laughter fill the air,
Bouncing boats without a care.

Paddle over to the stand,
Fruit-filled cups in every hand.
Syrup drips and laughter spills,
Tangerine dreams and citrus thrills.

Floating on a fruity float,
Jubilant, we happily gloat.
Grapefruits grin and nectarines shine,
In this fruity world, we're divine.

Donut-shaped delights abound,
Around each bend, joy is found.
With every bite, we raise a toast,
To the golden fruit we love most.

The Fruit-Filled Oasis

By the shore, where colors glow,
Banana boats in the flow.
Limes are dancing in the breeze,
Happiness grows like the trees.

Ladies donning fruity hats,
Coconut dreams and talkative cats.
Juices splash, what a sight!
Sparkly laughter, pure delight.

Berries bounce on the sand,
Squishy treats from foreign lands.
Mirthful moments, sweetened rays,
Solutions for our cloudy days.

In this oasis made of cheer,
Every moment's silk and clear.
Savor life with fruity flair,
Happiness is everywhere!

Summertime's Best Offerings

Sunshine gifts a juicy spread,
Watermelons, ripe and red.
Popsicles melt, a tasty mess,
While laughter reigns, who could guess?

Slathered in a tangy coat,
Sippin' smoothies, we gloat.
Nights of fruit, a merry tease,
Under stars, we swing with ease.

With every bite, a silly grin,
Peaches giggle, soakin' skin.
Tropical breezes, tales of old,
Friendship's worth more than gold.

In gatherings of vibrant hues,
Joyful hearts, with laughter, cruise.
This summer, with its playful swirls,
Best offerings, a fruity world.

Secrets of a Tropical Escape

In a land where the sun loves to bake,
The fruit wears a crown, make no mistake.
It winks in the breeze, with a laugh so loud,
Inviting the brave to join its crowd.

The sand tickles toes, the waves play fetch,
But watch out for seagulls, they'll make a sketch!
With tropical drinks that dance and sway,
You might end up singing the night away.

Beneath palm trees swaying, life's a joke,
You'll trip on a coconut, no need to poke!
With laughter so sweet, and joy on display,
Each moment feels like a grand cabaret.

So grab a bright hat, and don't be shy,
In this secret escape, the good vibes fly!
With flavors so wild and sights that gleam,
You'll find it's a paradise, or just a dream!

Nectar of the Gods

In a cup made of laughter and sunbeam spark,
Lies a potion where sweet meets the dark.
Sip it slowly, let giggles arise,
For this drink wears a mask of surprise.

It's golden and sticky, with bubbles that pop,
When you take a big swig, you might just stop!
You'll dance like a mango under the sun,
Announcing to all that you're here just for fun.

Add a tiny umbrella, make it a show,
And toast to the sunshine, let your worries go.
With friends in bright shirts and laughter so grand,
This nectar we share is simply unplanned!

We sip and we spill, like juice on our chin,
In this fruity concoction, everyone wins.
So come chase the giggles, grab a cool glass,
And let the good vibes forever amass!

Radiant Gardens Await

In a garden where rubies and gold intertwine,
You'll giggle with blooms, cascading like wine.
A fruit basket grows with colors so bright,
Every turn brings a chuckle, a delightful sight.

The butterflies twirl with a jazz in their step,
While fruits form a band, oh, a wild prep!
From prickly to juicy, they dance in a line,
You might just join in, feel free to recline.

But watch out for the bees, they're quite the jest,
With honeyed ambitions, they're having the best.
Gathering laughter beneath sunny skies,
Every flower a joke, every leaf a surprise.

So roam through this haven, let joy cascade,
In radiant gardens, where memories are made.
With bright laughs and giggles, life's simply a play,
In this wild, wacky, fruity ballet!

The Fruit of Serenity

Beneath a sky of candy floss blue,
Lies a treasure not many pursue.
With humor and bliss, it beckons the bold,
The secret to joy, more precious than gold.

In the shade of tall palms, a picnic's delight,
With friends and some snacks, it feels just right.
A slice of sweet laughter, a dollop of fun,
Life's simple joys shine as bright as the sun.

As giggles erupt like fizz in a cup,
You'll dance with the coconuts, hold your chin up!
With each fruity bite, let your worries flee,
For in this bright moment, we're forever free.

So gather around, let the good times sprout,
In the fruit of this laughter, wipe away doubt.
With sunshine and smiles, let's raise our cheer,
For every sweet moment, let's hold it near!

Lush Harmony of the Tropics

In a land where jokes come sweet,
A fruit with spikes can't be beat.
Wobbling laughter fills the air,
As fruity friends dance without a care.

Sunshine smiles from leafy trees,
While critters giggle in the breeze.
A jester's hat, a yellow hue,
Tales of joy in sunsets too!

Bouncing thoughts like juicy drops,
Tropical punchline never stops.
A slip on peel, oh what a sight,
Laughter ringing day and night.

Twirling flavors with a cheer,
Sipping sunshine, oh so dear.
Nature's giggle in every bite,
A party under stars so bright.

The Golden Crown's Song

A fruit with style, it wears a crown,
Mischief swirling in its gown.
Jokes about its regal form,
In sunshine's glow, it's the norm.

Golden laughter fills the feast,
While jungle critters join the least.
With every slice, a giggle sings,
Jumpy joy from summer flings.

Sipping nectar, a sticky treat,
Ticklish taste in every beat.
Bouncing rhythms, fruity tunes,
Dancing under lazy moons.

So gather round, let laughter flow,
In crown and cheer, let spirits grow.
The world turns bright with every joke,
Around the fruit, the laughter's woke.

Tropical Echoes in the Breeze

Waves of laughter on the shore,
Golden echoes, wanting more.
Tickling air and fruity fun,
Banter shines like morning sun.

In the fronds, jokes take flight,
Critters giggling, pure delight.
With each breeze, silly rhymes,
Tropical tales of playful times.

Sipping sprites from nature's cup,
Cheeky smiles in bright-up beats up.
A fruity feast full of glee,
Happiness in every tree.

So let the laughter bloom so wild,
With nature's humor, we're all a child.
Together we'll dance in joyous spree,
Echoes of fun through land and sea.

Nectar of Elation

Sweetness drips with every bite,
Joyful giggles take flight.
With golden juice that tickles the tongue,
Even the frogs are singing their song.

Jumpy sirens of fruity fun,
Under the gaze of a cheeky sun.
A silly splash, a sticky slip,
Laughter pours from every sip.

Tropical shenanigans at play,
Golden smiles light the way.
The nectar flows, a bubbly stream,
Bubbling joy, like a daydream.

So gather friends, let laughter soar,
In this land of jest, you'll want more.
With every bite, a chuckle grows,
Beneath the trees, where laughter flows.

Rays of Sunshine and Sweetness

In a jungle dressed in green,
Laughter bubbles, oh what a scene!
Fruits in hats, dancing with glee,
A feast awaits by the palm tree.

Juggling coconuts, what a sight,
Happiness blooms from morning till night!
Bumblebees buzzing, they join the cheer,
Sippin' nectar, no worries here.

Sandy friends in sunglasses bright,
Flip-flops clapping, oh what delight!
The sun's a comedian, making us grin,
With every giggle, our joy begins.

A tropical soiree, drinks by the pool,
Twirling and spinning, what a fine rule!
This paradise sparkles, full of surprise,
As laughter and sunshine intertwine and rise.

A Journey to Tropical Bliss

Pack your bags, we're headed for fun,
To a land where the laughter's never done!
Watermelons rollerskating by,
Leaping papayas, oh my, oh my!

Follow the path where the giggles bloom,
To a castle made of coconut and loom.
Mangoes in capes, they sway and parade,
In this silly land, worries do fade.

Hammocks are singing, swaying with grace,
As the breeze tickles your happy face.
A conga line of zany fruit,
Join them now, don't dare to be mute!

Every corner glints with a smile,
Delightful shenanigans stretching for miles.
So grab a slice of joy, let it unfold,
In this journey, pure laughter behold!

The Harmony of Flavor and Sun

Under the sun, bananas do groove,
Swaying gently in a glorious move.
Lemonade rivers, sparkling bright,
Sipping joy, from morning till night.

Kiwi and berry, a colorful dance,
Mixing together in a fruity romance.
Jokes in the air like bubbles on shore,
Every giggle calls for just one scoop more!

Cherries in hats, they jam to the beat,
Finding their rhythm in this fruity street.
With every bite, there comes a cheer,
The flavors unite, spreading good vibes near.

So let's twirl and whirl, all day in the sun,
In this harmony of laughter, we're all so young!
Here in the tropics, oh what a find,
A world bursting with joy, and fruit intertwined.

Unveiling Nature's Golden Secrets

In the garden of giggles, sweet secrets reside,
Fruits wearing crowns, they take you for a ride.
Giggling grapes tell tales of delight,
Berry bush whispers secrets at night.

The ground is a canvas, painted with cheer,
As fruits cluster closer, all drawing near.
Jolly oranges bounce on warm sand,
Sharing their laughter across the land.

The sun winks down, tickling the leaves,
With every rustle, nature believes.
In this sweet garden where flavors collide,
Unraveling secrets makes hearts swell with pride.

So grab your friends, join the fun parade,
In this golden ballet of joy unmade.
With every crunch and every slurp,
Nature reveals the joy that does erupt!

Serendipity in the Heart of Summer

Under the sun, a dance begins,
A hula skirt and silly grins,
We laugh and sway, no care in sight,
Juicy dreams take joyful flight.

With every splash, the giggles rise,
As globs of fruit wear spiky eyes,
A fruity feast, no forks allowed,
We're all just kids, and oh, so loud!

Sand between toes and juice on hands,
Lemons bounce like rubber bands,
Tanned and sticky, we run and twirl,
In the heart of summer, we whirl!

So raise your glass, let's make a toast,
To silly days we love the most,
With quirky friends, and sun-kissed skin,
In this delight, let's all dive in!

Where Warmth Meets the Ocean

Waves of laughter crash with glee,
Sharing secrets with the sea,
Sunburnt noses, a goofy joke,
Magical times, in sun we soak.

Floppy hats and sunglasses bright,
Sipping smoothies, what a sight!
The seagulls scream, as if to tease,
Eating chips while chilling with ease.

The ocean whispers, "Come and play!"
"Don't juggle fruits? You'll be okay!"
Caught in waves, we start to spin,
Making memories buried within.

Lay on the sand, feel a cool breeze,
While fruity dreams are sure to please,
With every wave, let's ride the fun,
In warmth where laughter has begun!

Lush Landscapes of Flavor

In a jungle of colors, we wander free,
With tickling taste buds, just you and me,
Swing from the branches, grab a delight,
Eating sweetness both day and night.

Silly critters peek from the vines,
Poking fun at our fruity designs,
A smoothie river flows past our toes,
As laughter dances, and off it goes.

Tropical breezes carry our cheers,
While flavor explosions ring in our ears,
Chasing fruits, we leap and glide,
In lush landscapes where fun won't hide.

Tarzan calls out; we can't say no,
As laughter transforms into a fun show,
With juiciness dripping, we claim our space,
Where smiles bloom with tasty grace!

The Enchantment of Fruity Shores

Magic kisses from the dew,
Where fruity dreams come fresh and true,
Tickled toes in sandy bliss,
A laughter-filled, frosty kiss.

Beneath palm trees, jokes collide,
With every sip, we feel that ride,
Fruity waves crash on our hearts,
As sun-kissed joy in summer starts.

Sandcastles fashioned like sweet treats,
In this land where flavor meets,
A jester's hat, a splash, a scream,
Together we float in a fruity dream!

So dance with pineapples, join the fray,
In this enchanting, wacky way,
Let's find delight in this grand race,
As fruity shores become our space!

www.ingramcontent.com/pod-product-compliance
Lightning Source LLC
Chambersburg PA
CBHW060114230426
43661CB00003B/182